57099916R00054

Made in United States
North Haven, CT
06 September 2024

PRACTICE READING & WRITING FROM RIGHT TO LEFT

THIS WORKBOOK BELONGS TO

....

....

....

....

COMPLETE ALL YOUR
READING & WRITING SKILLS

Congratulations on taking the first step on your Hebrew journey! You are now officially on the road to reading and writing in Hebrew like a native, and I'm thrilled to be here as your guide. **I've handcrafted a comprehensive curriculum** for you, where each step is carefully designed to enhance your reading and writing skills in Hebrew, building upon the previous one. Following these steps using my tried-and-true methods, you'll be reading and writing in Hebrew in no time:

STEP 1: PRINT LETTERS
The first step you've already started is this Hebrew 1 Workbook! It teaches you how to write in Hebrew using the Print alphabet letters and provides all the essential basics you need to start writing in Hebrew.

STEP 2: CURSIVE/SCRIPT LETTERS
Once you've completed Hebrew 1, the Hebrew 2 Workbook will perfect your writing skills with graceful Cursive/Script letters. **Before you dive into Hebrew 1, make sure you have Hebrew 2 handy and ready** to start as you complete Hebrew 1. Starting Hebrew 2 right after you've completed this workbook is my tested recipe for quick results, avoiding frustration, and being fully prepared for the next exciting steps in your Hebrew journey.

Starting with Print letters is a smart move! They're easier to learn and will make Hebrew 2 much easier to navigate and complete. Plus, once you know your Print letters, you'll be able to read anything printed—books, the Bible, news, TV subtitles, street signs—you name it! Cursive/Script letters are equally important as they're the form used for handwriting in Hebrew, appearing on products, in ads, and becoming your go-to method of writing as you advance in Hebrew (and as a native speaker).

STEP 3: THE VOWEL NIKUD SYSTEM
Hebrew 1 & 2 will complete all your writing skills in Hebrew. Hebrew 3 will complete your reading skills as well, teaching you the vowel Nikud system. Once you've completed all three steps, you'll have all the tools you need to practice your way into reading and writing in Hebrew like a pro.

To order Hebrew 2 & 3 locally go to HEBREWBYINBAL.COM/ORDER, click on the book image, and scroll to your country/area.

Your excited Hebrew journey guide,

Inbal Amit

HOW TO MAKE THE MOST OUT OF YOUR WORKBOOK?

First thing's first: Make sure to watch the videos I've created for you as you go through this workbook. You'll learn how to write and sound each letter, master the PSP (Phonetic System for Pronunciation), and more. **Go to HEBREWBYINBAL.COM/ORDER, and click on the video** to watch the "Hebrew 1, 2, 3, Coloring Books & Notebooks" playlist on my YouTube channel.

If you're a young learner, grab an adult to guide you through the process and help make sure everything clicks. And don't forget to add some color to each letter and its corresponding illustration for extra fun.

The next page shows you all the treasures you get to master each letter - think of it as a roadmap to discovering all the delights of this workbook!

When it comes to Hebrew, **reading and writing go from right to left.** Don't worry, your trusty workbook is here to help you make this transition with ease. The helpful arrows and text throughout this workbook will guide you as you adapt to this different writing style.

Each letter is taught using familiar English words that are widely used by Hebrew speakers and Israelis just as you're using them or almost the same, making it a breeze to learn and remember the new letters and their sounds.

Tracing is key to writing Hebrew letters correctly. Trace by following the middle line of each letter, not its outline. And remember, there's a specific direction and sequence to writing in Hebrew that you'll find in the workbook using arrows and numbers.

After tracing each letter or word on two pages, it's time to put your newfound skills to the test with some freehand writing. The spaces between the traced letters are perfect for that. For extra practice, trace with a pencil, erase, and trace again, and use the extra pages at the end of this workbook.

Got a question? I'm here to help. Send me an email at hi@hebrewbyinbal.com.

A SAMPLE OF EACH LETTER PAGE

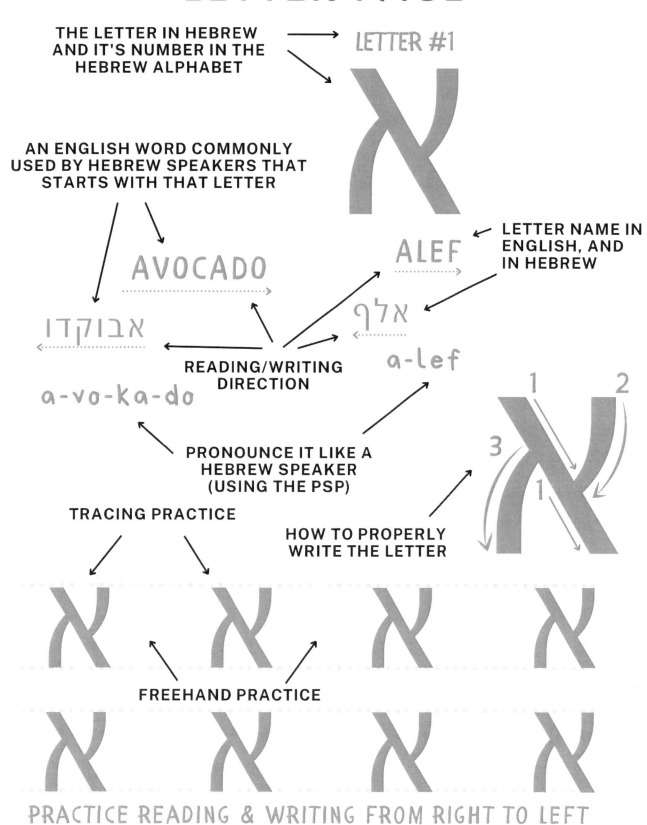

THE LETTER IN HEBREW AND IT'S NUMBER IN THE HEBREW ALPHABET

LETTER #1

AN ENGLISH WORD COMMONLY USED BY HEBREW SPEAKERS THAT STARTS WITH THAT LETTER

LETTER NAME IN ENGLISH, AND IN HEBREW

ALEF

AVOCADO

אלף

אבוקדו

a-lef

READING/WRITING DIRECTION

a-vo-ka-do

PRONOUNCE IT LIKE A HEBREW SPEAKER (USING THE PSP)

TRACING PRACTICE

HOW TO PROPERLY WRITE THE LETTER

FREEHAND PRACTICE

PRACTICE READING & WRITING FROM RIGHT TO LEFT

HEY THERE!
I HOPE YOU'RE
EXCITED

You are about to explore the Hebrew language!

Hebrew is T-rex-level cool, being a super ancient language that is now a mix of ancient and modern

What if I were to tell you that you already know at least 20 words in Hebrew?

Well, it's true! For each letter, you will discover a word you know how to say PERFECTLY in Hebrew

THINGS TO KNOW ABOUT LETTER SHAPES

Hebrew has two types of letters: Print and Script/cursive.
In the next pages you will learn the Print letters, which are straight lined

Letters have many styles and shapes (called fonts). This can be a bit confusing when you're just starting to learn the language

That is why the letter shape (font) you will learn here is super easy and practical.

If you see any differences between the letter at the top of the page and the letter at the bottom to trace, don't worry. It's ok. Just follow the instructions

ALEF

אלף　'a-lef

AVOCADO

אבוקדו

a-vo-'ka-do

PRACTICE READING & WRITING FROM RIGHT TO LEFT

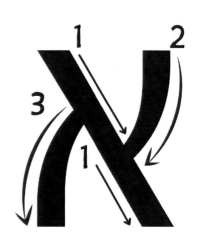

BET

בית bet

BANANA

בננה

ba-'na-nah

1

2

3

PRACTICE READING & WRITING FROM RIGHT TO LEFT

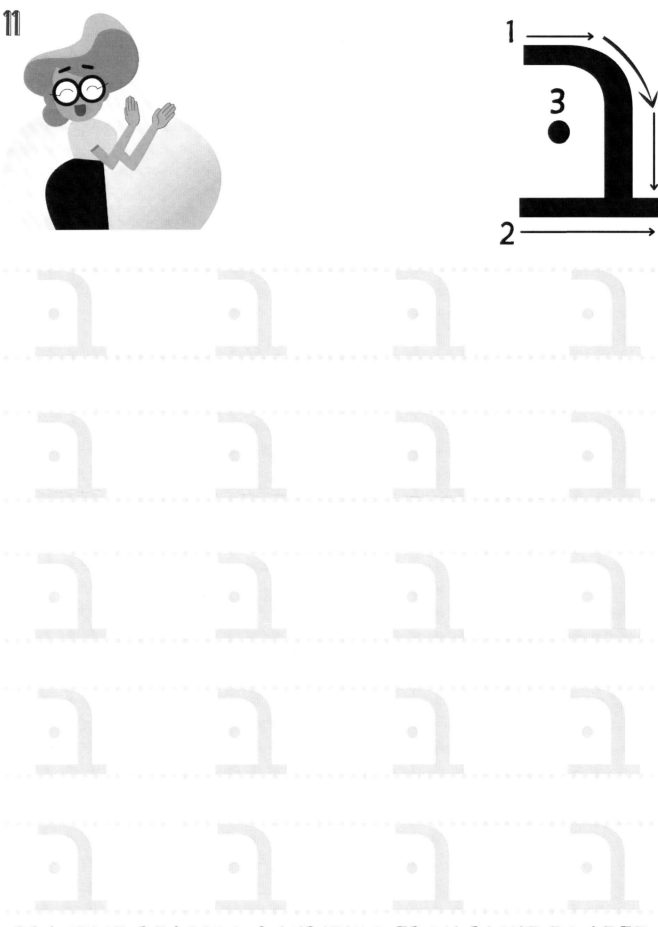

11

THINGS TO KNOW ABOUT

בּ

BET

The letter BET has a variation called VET when you take off the dot in the middle

ב

VET

VET sounds like the English letter V as in the words Van and Vacation

There are 3 letters in Hebrew with and without a dot/Dugesh (pronounced da-'gesh).

We mark them with a heart.

When each of these 3 letters have a dot, we say "With a Dugesh". When the dot is removed, we say "No Dugesh"

YOUR FIRST WORD IN HEBREW

let's put together the first two letters ALEF and BET (with a Dugesh) to write the word DAD in Hebrew:

א בָּא

Say it in Hebrew: 'a-ba

אבא   אבא

PRACTICE READING & WRITING FROM RIGHT TO LEFT

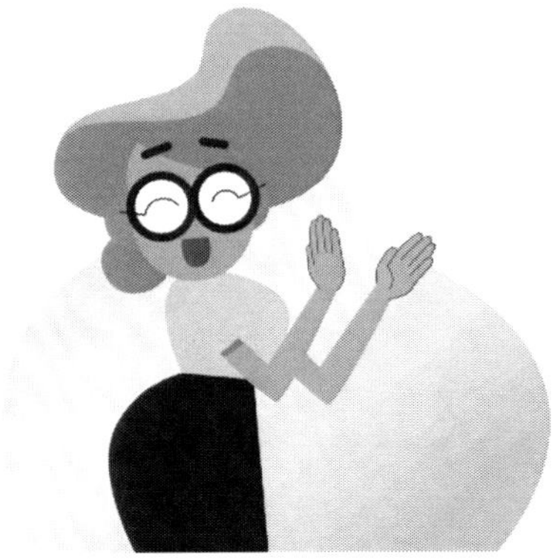

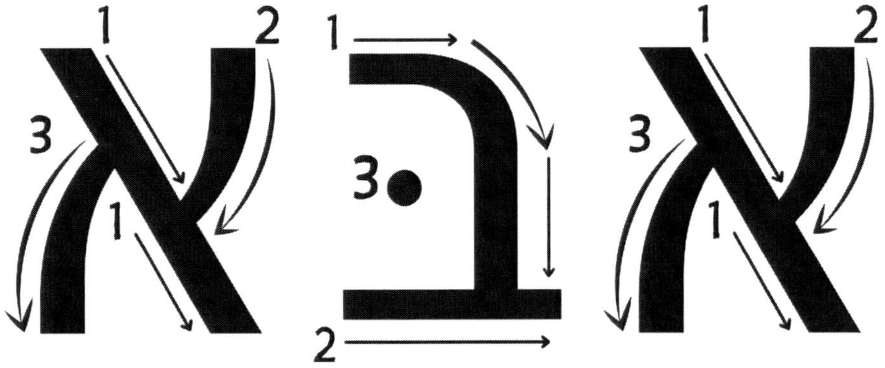

אבּא אבּא

אבּא אבּא

אבּא אבּא

אבּא אבּא

אבּא אבּא

PRACTICE READING & WRITING FROM RIGHT TO LEFT

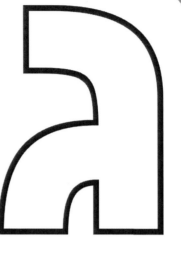

GIMEL

גימל

'gee-mel

GOAL

גול

gol

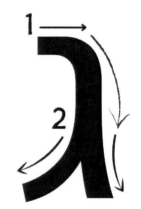

גּ   גּ   גּ   גּ

גּ   גּ   גּ   גּ

PRACTICE READING & WRITING FROM RIGHT TO LEFT

GIMEL ALWAYS MAKES A
SOUND AS IN THE WORD
GUITAR.
GIMEL WRITTEN WITH A '
SIGN MAKES A SOUND AS
IS THE WORD GENTLE

PRACTICE READING & WRITING FROM RIGHT TO LEFT

DALET

דלת ˈda-let

DOLPHIN

דולפין

dol-ˈfeen

1

2

PRACTICE READING & WRITING FROM RIGHT TO LEFT

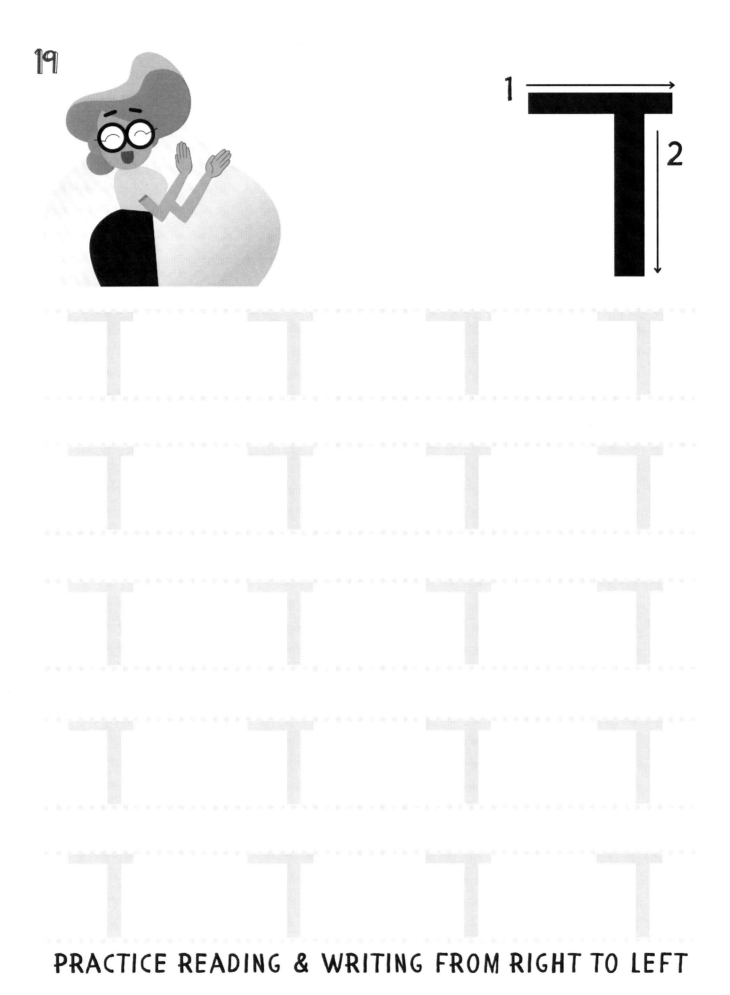

PRACTICE READING & WRITING FROM RIGHT TO LEFT

YOUR SECOND WORD IN HEBREW

Now let's put together the forth and third letters DALET and GIMEL to write the word FISH in Hebrew:

דג

Say it in Hebrew: dag

דג   דג

PRACTICE READING & WRITING FROM RIGHT TO LEFT

21

PRACTICE READING & WRITING FROM RIGHT TO LEFT

22

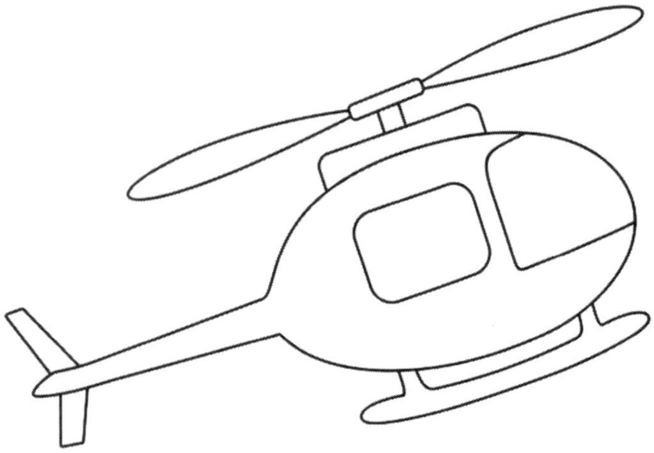

ה

HE / HEY

הא   he / hey

HELICOPTER

הליקופטר

he-lee-'kop-ter

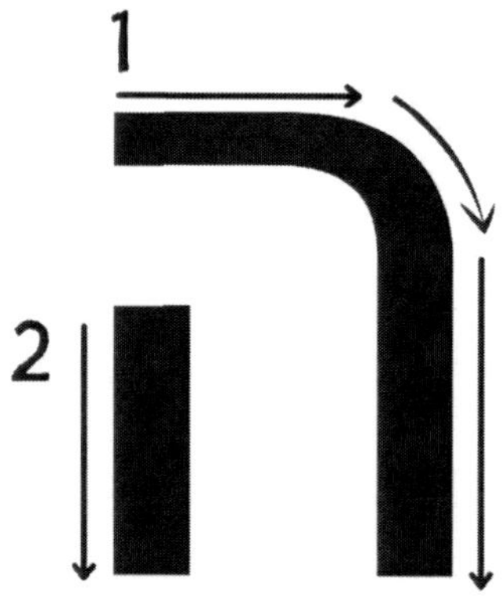

1

2

ה

ה ה ה ה

ה ה ה ה

PRACTICE READING & WRITING FROM RIGHT TO LEFT

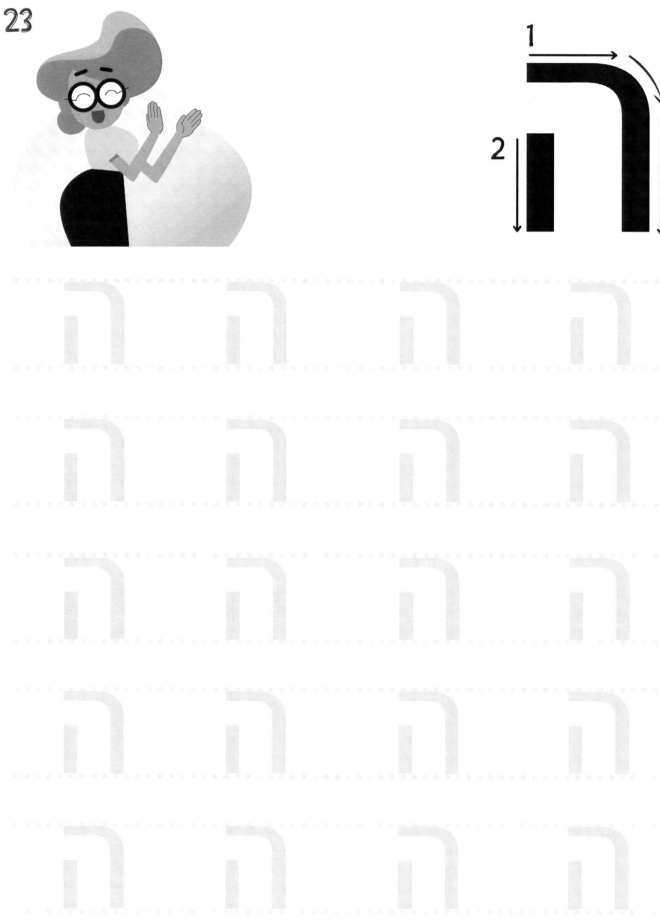

23

PRACTICE READING & WRITING FROM RIGHT TO LEFT

VAV

·······>

‖ vav

<····

VIRUS

·······>

וירוס

<·······>

'vee-roos

1

PRACTICE READING & WRITING FROM RIGHT TO LEFT

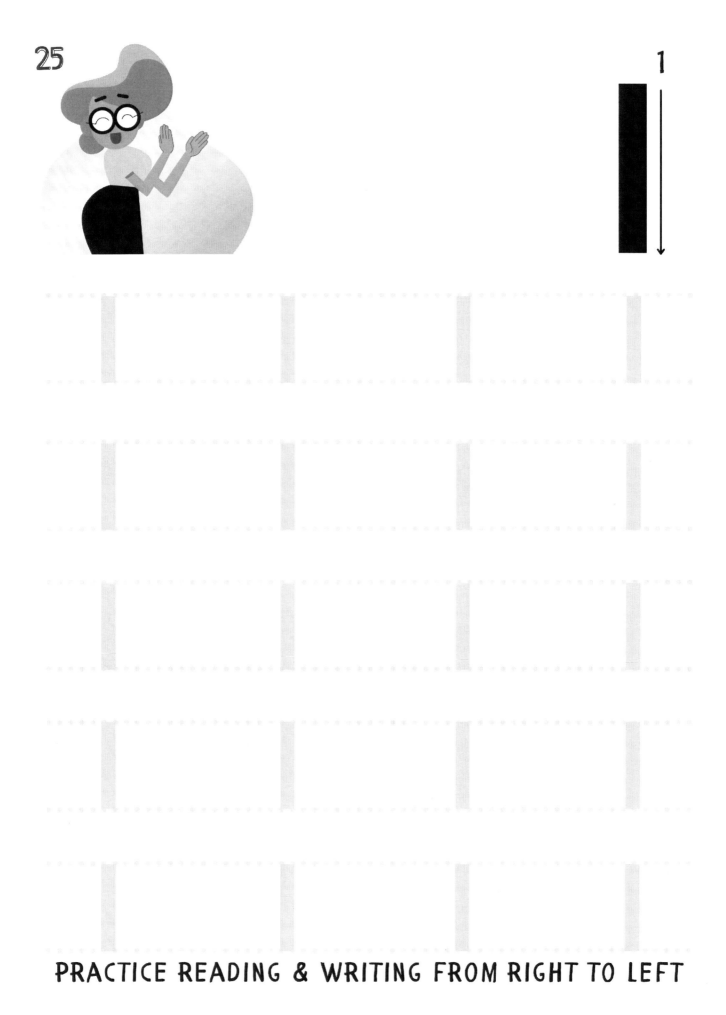

PRACTICE READING & WRITING FROM RIGHT TO LEFT

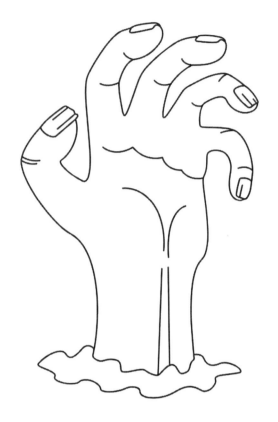

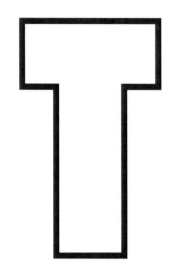

ZAYIN

זַיִן 'za-yeen

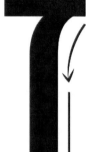

ZOMBIE

זוֹמְבִּי

'zom-bee

PRACTICE READING & WRITING FROM RIGHT TO LEFT

27

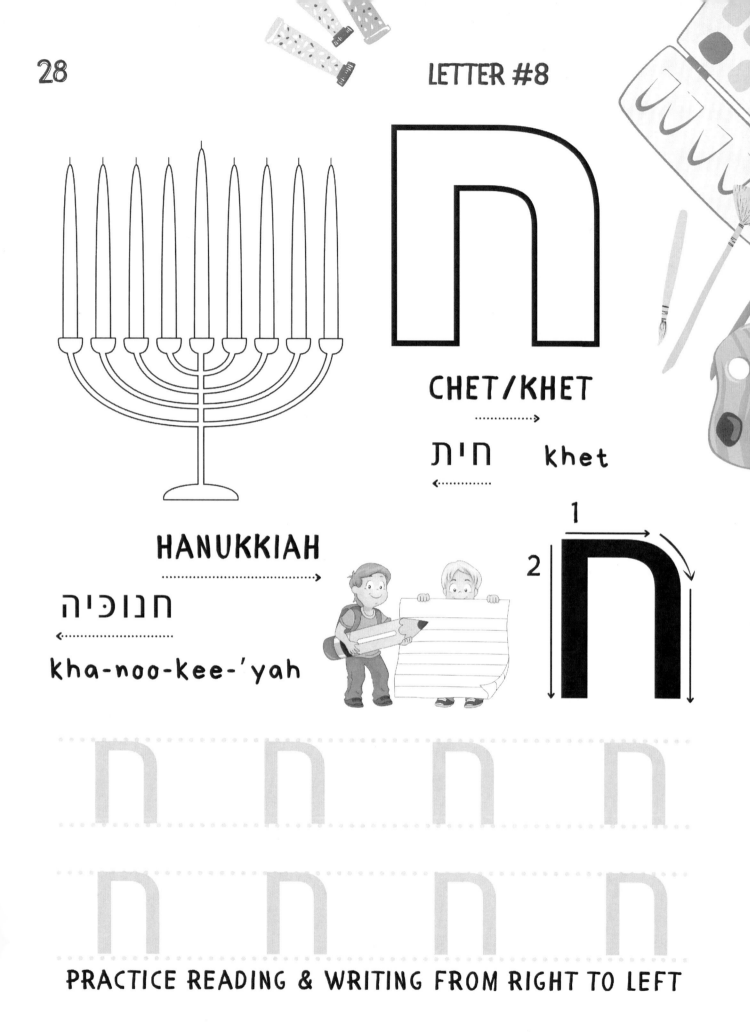

CHET/KHET

חית   khet

HANUKKIAH

חנוכיה

kha-noo-kee-'yah

1
2

PRACTICE READING & WRITING FROM RIGHT TO LEFT

THINGS TO KNOW ABOUT

ח
Chet/Khet

KHET is one of a couple of letters in Hebrew that do not have a same sound-making letter in English.

Another word in Hebrew starting with KHET ח and makes a KHET sound is Challah: kha-'lah חלה

KHET is sometimes written in English with an H or Ch. Because it makes a different sound than Ch or H, we use Kh to write it in English

Let's practice writing the letter KHET ח

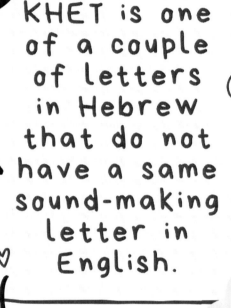

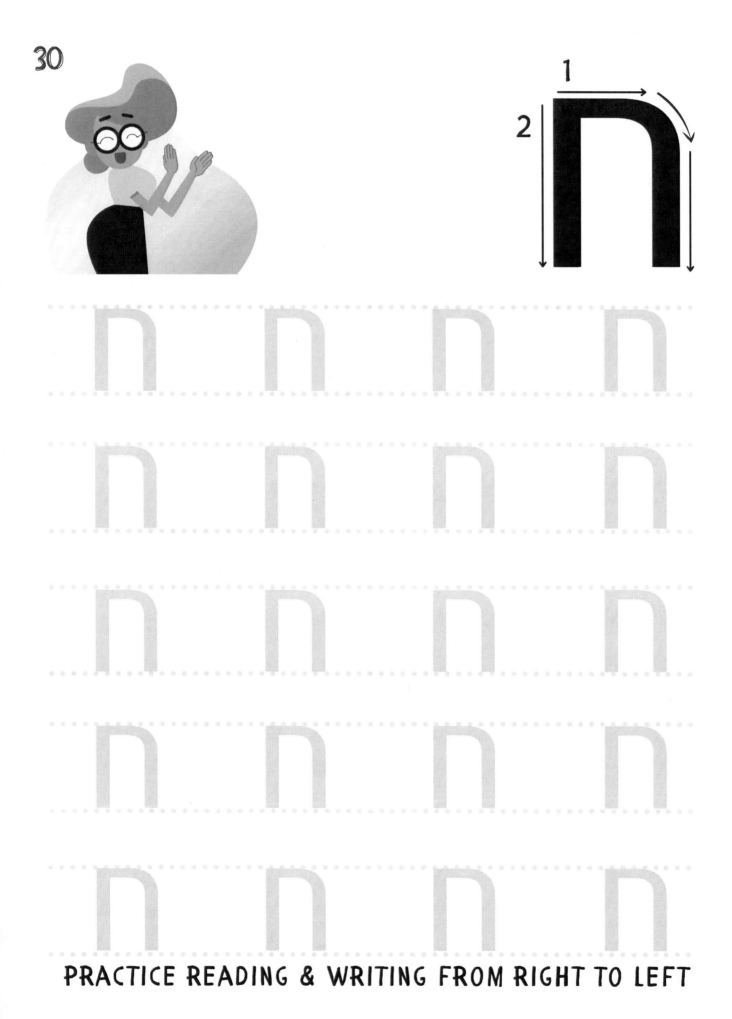

PRACTICE READING & WRITING FROM RIGHT TO LEFT

YOUR THIRD WORD IN HEBREW

let's put together
the letters ALEF and KHET
to write the word
BROTHER in Hebrew:

אח

Say it in Hebrew: akh

אח אח

PRACTICE READING & WRITING FROM RIGHT TO LEFT

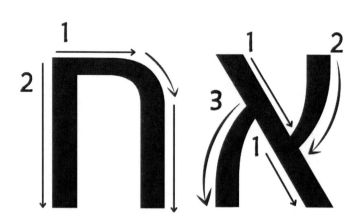

אֵת

אֵת אֵת

אֵת אֵת

אֵת אֵת

אֵת אֵת

PRACTICE READING & WRITING FROM RIGHT TO LEFT

I Hope You're Loving Your Workbook

Can I ask you to take 60 seconds to review it?

Your review is the most helpful feedback for me as the author, and for others just like you looking for Hebrew resources.

Toda Rabah - thank you so much!

WHERE TO SUBMIT YOUR REVIEW?

Scan this, OR:

If you ordered the workbook: On your Amazon orders tap the workbook › Scroll to 'How's your item?" › Tap "Write a review".

If you ordered OR were gifted the workbook: Search "Hebrew by Inbal" on Amazon › tap on the Workbook › scroll to "Customer Review" › tap "Write a Review".

TET

טית   tet

TRACTOR

טרקטור

t-'rak-tor

1

PRACTICE READING & WRITING FROM RIGHT TO LEFT

PRACTICE READING & WRITING FROM RIGHT TO LEFT

YOD

·······►

יוד · · · · · yod

◄·······

YOGURT

·······►

יוגורט

◄·······

'yo-goor-t

1

PRACTICE READING & WRITING FROM RIGHT TO LEFT

1

GREAT JOB! YOU ALREADY KNOW TEN LETTERS!

READ THEM IN ORDER – FROM RIGHT TO LEFT

ד 4	ג 3	ב 2 (with heart)	בּ 2	א 1
DALET DOLPHIN	GIMEL GOAL	VET (NO DOT)	BET BANANA	ALEF AVOCADO

ט 9	ח 8	ז 7	ו 6	ה 5
TET TRACTOR	KHET HANUKKIAH	ZAYIN ZOMBIE	VAV VIRUS	HE/HEY HELICOPTER

י 10
YOD YOGURT

LETTER WITH NO DUGESH (DOT REMOVED) ♡

PRACTICE YOUR LETTERS
IT'S OK TO GO BACK AND LOOK

page 10

write the
letter BET
(with a Dugesh)
here

page 22

write the
letter HEY
here

page 31

write the word
BROTHER (AKH
in Hebrew)
here

KAF

כף   kaf

CABLE

כבל

'ka-bel

1
2

PRACTICE READING & WRITING FROM RIGHT TO LEFT

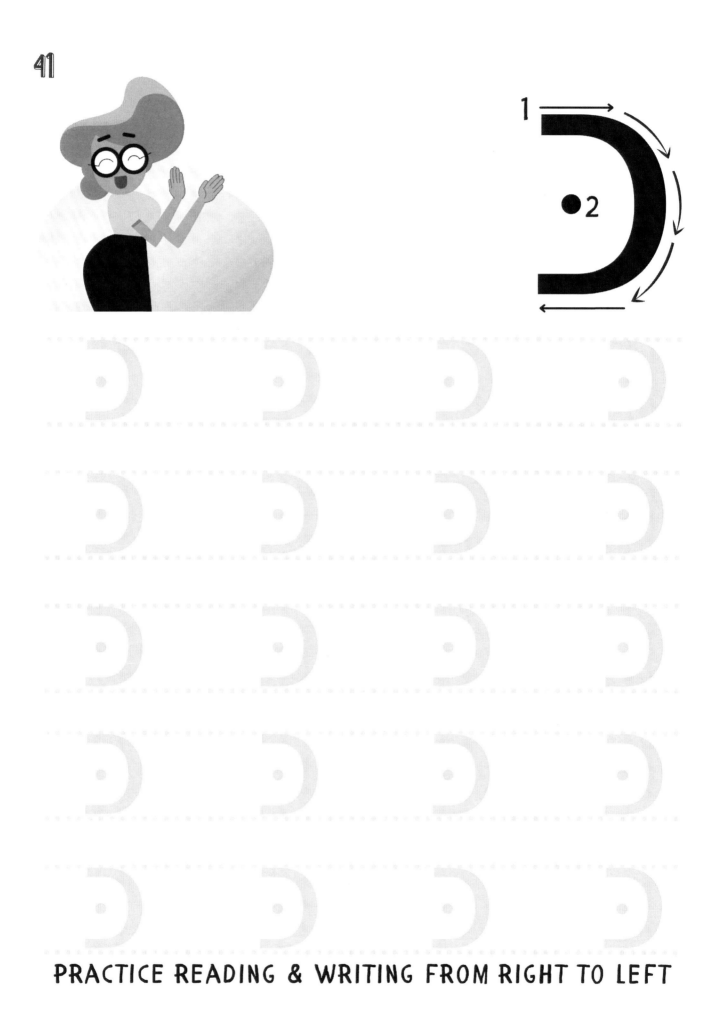

PRACTICE READING & WRITING FROM RIGHT TO LEFT

THINGS TO KNOW ABOUT

כ

KAF

KAF is the second letter with a no Dugesh variation, called KHAF

כ KHAF

KHAF (No Dugesh = dot removed) makes a sound much like the letter KHET ח you already know

Let's practice writing כ KHAF

Because of that, KHAF כ SOUNDS like the first letter in the words Challah and Hanukkah (WRITTEN in Hebrew with a KHET ח)

43

KAF becomes KHAF by taking off the dot (Dugesh) in the middle. This is how we write KHAF = KAF with no Dugesh

1

PRACTICE READING & WRITING FROM RIGHT TO LEFT

THINGS TO KNOW ABOUT

כ

At the end of a word, the letter KHAF (no Dugesh = no dot) is written ך

KHAF at the end of a word is called KHAF SOFIT (khaf so-'feet). SOFIT is the female form of the word End

The sound of of כ KHAF does not change at the end of a word, only how it is written

We mark letters that are written different at the end of the word with a diamond

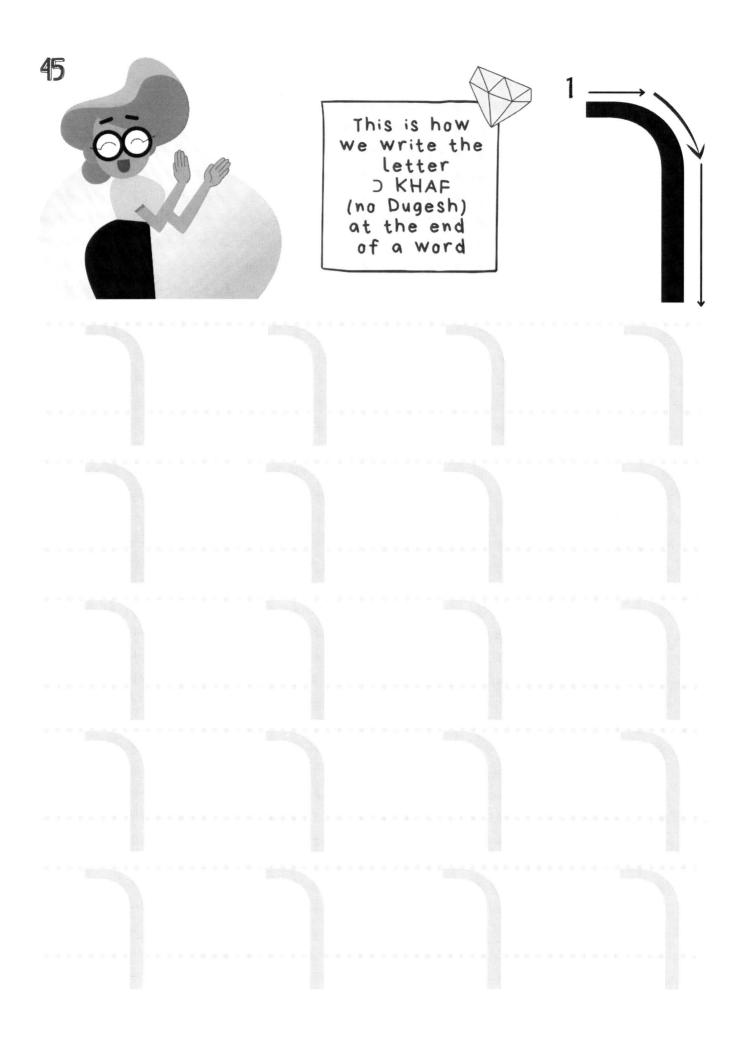

This is how we write the letter ך KHAF (no Dugesh) at the end of a word

LETTER #12

LEMON

לימון

lee-'mon

LAMED

למד   'la-med

1

PRACTICE READING & WRITING FROM RIGHT TO LEFT

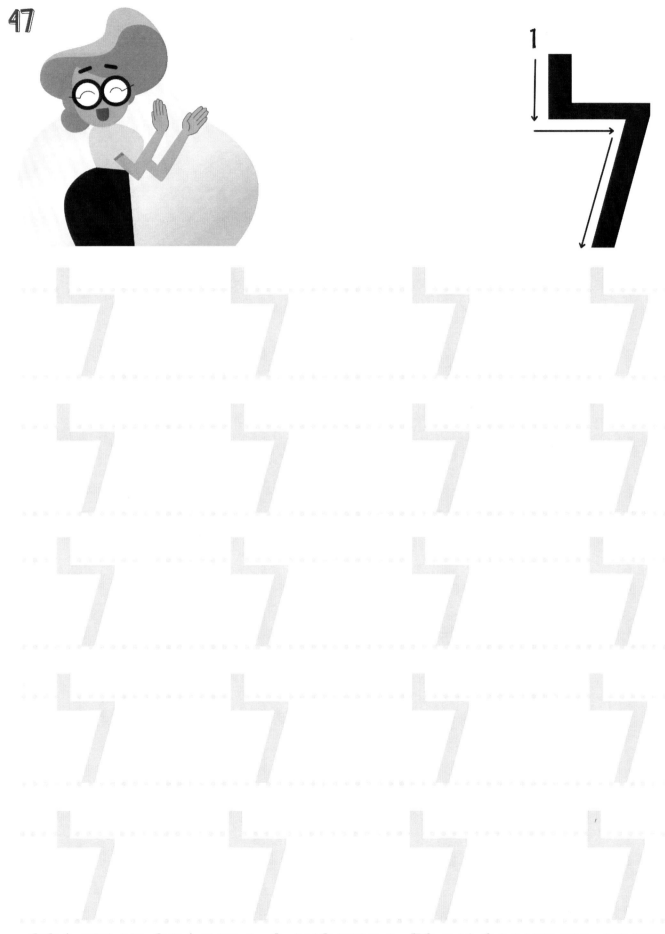

PRACTICE READING & WRITING FROM RIGHT TO LEFT

YOUR NEXT WORD IN HEBREW

Now let's put together the letters KAF, LAMED, and VET (BET with no Dugesh) to write the word DOG in Hebrew:

כֶּלֶב

Say it in Hebrew: 'ke-lev

כלב כלב

PRACTICE READING & WRITING FROM RIGHT TO LEFT

49

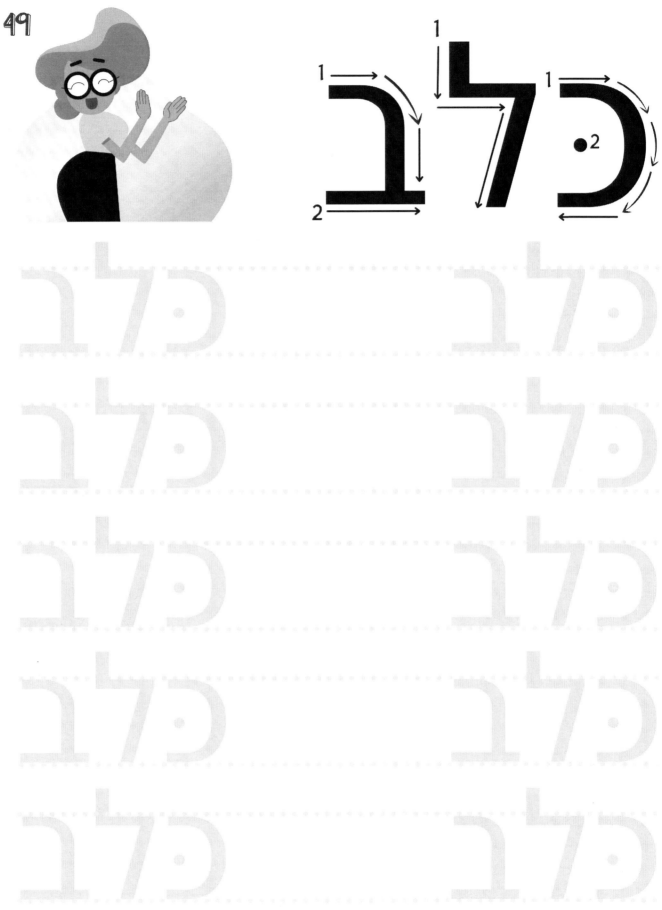

PRACTICE READING & WRITING FROM RIGHT TO LEFT

LETTER #13

מ

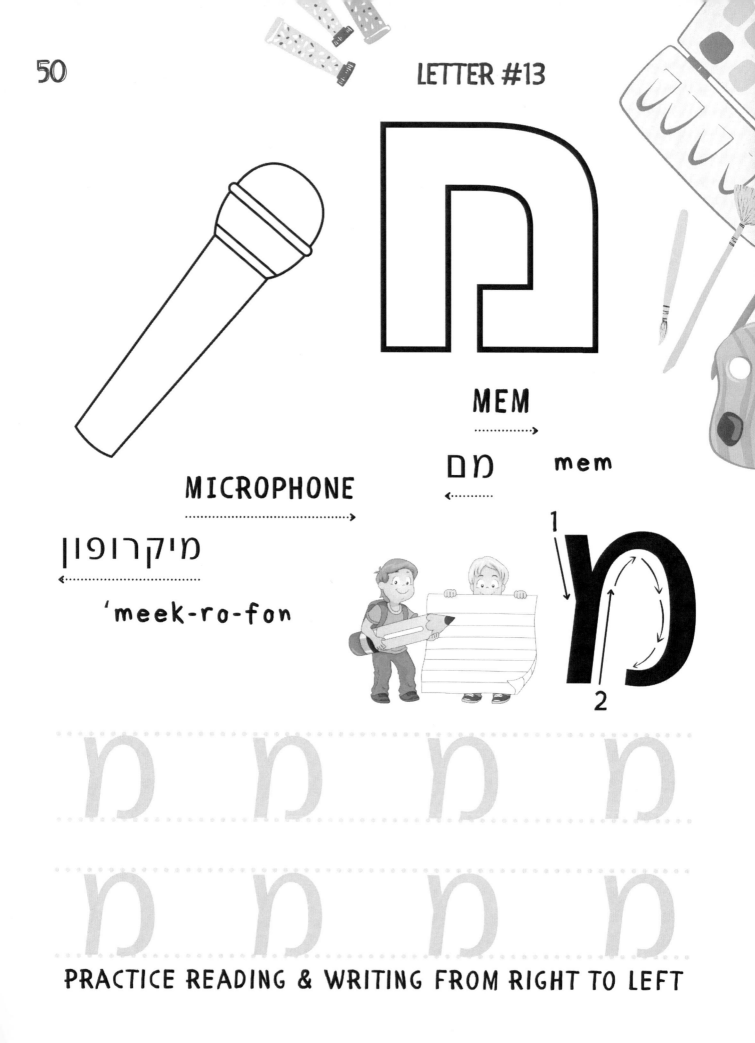

MEM

מם

mem

MICROPHONE

מיקרופון

'meek-ro-fon

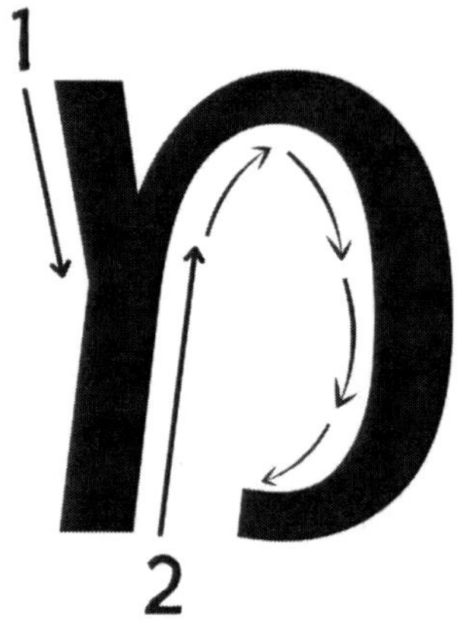

מ מ מ מ

מ מ מ מ

PRACTICE READING & WRITING FROM RIGHT TO LEFT

PRACTICE READING & WRITING FROM RIGHT TO LEFT

THINGS TO KNOW ABOUT

מ

MEM at the end of a word is written

ם

MEM at the end of a word is called MEM SOFIT (mem so-'feet)

The sound of of the the letter מ MEM does not change at the end of a word, only how it is written

Let's practice writing ם

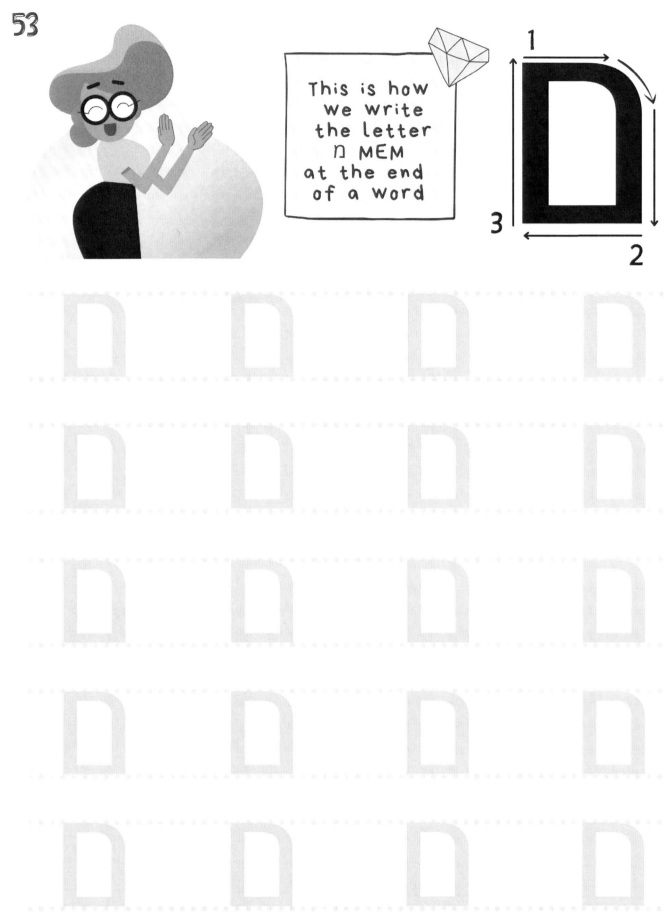

This is how we write the letter ם MEM at the end of a word

PRACTICE READING & WRITING FROM RIGHT TO LEFT

LETTER #14

ב

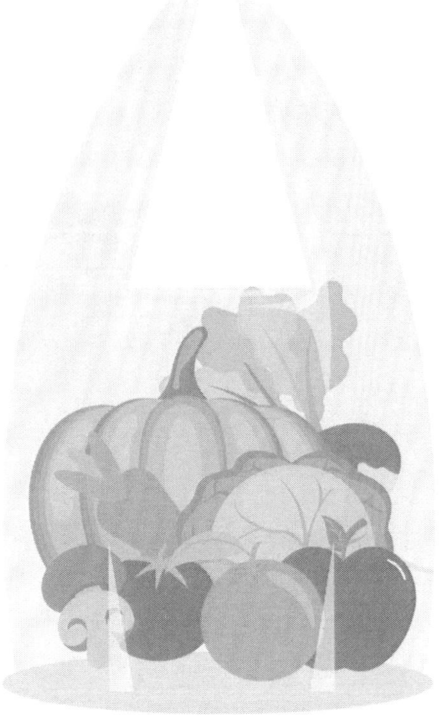

NUN

┘┌ ב   noon

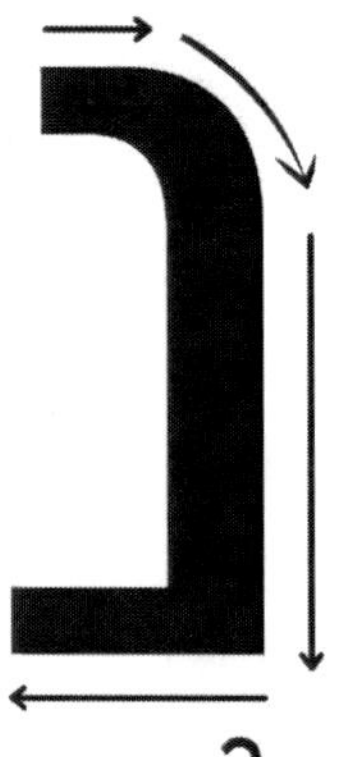

NYLON

ניילון

'nay-lon

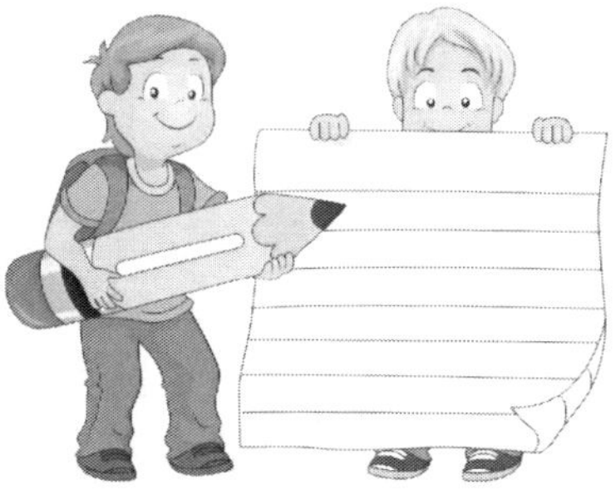

1

2

PRACTICE READING & WRITING FROM RIGHT TO LEFT

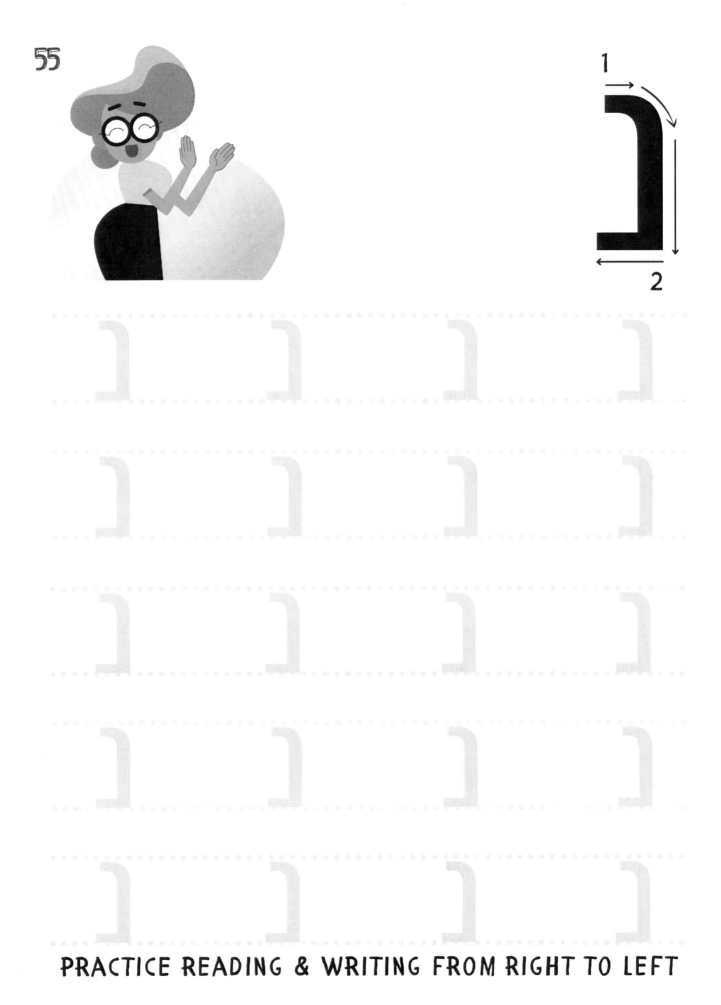

PRACTICE READING & WRITING FROM RIGHT TO LEFT

THINGS TO KNOW ABOUT

ן

NUN at the end of a word is written

ן

NUN at the end of a word is called NUN SOFIT (noon so-feet)

The sound of of letter ן NUN does not change at the end of a word, only how it is written

Let's practice writing ן

57

1

PRACTICE READING & WRITING FROM RIGHT TO LEFT

YOUR NEXT WORD IN HEBREW

Now let's put together the letters BET (with a Dugesh) and NUN SOFIT to write the word SON / BOY in Hebrew:

בֶּן

Say it in Hebrew: ben

בֶּן   בֶּן   בֶּן

PRACTICE READING & WRITING FROM RIGHT TO LEFT

59

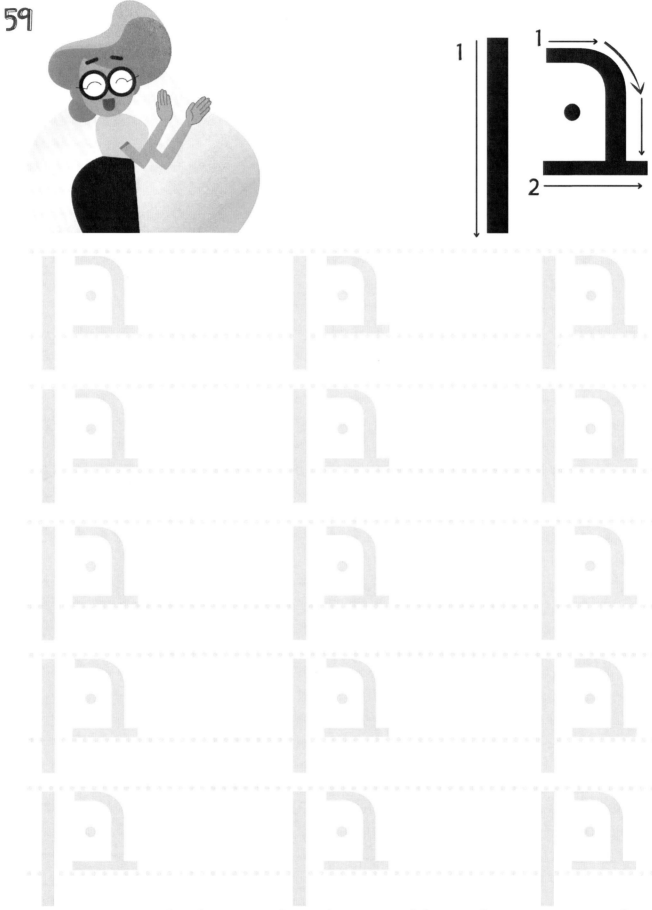

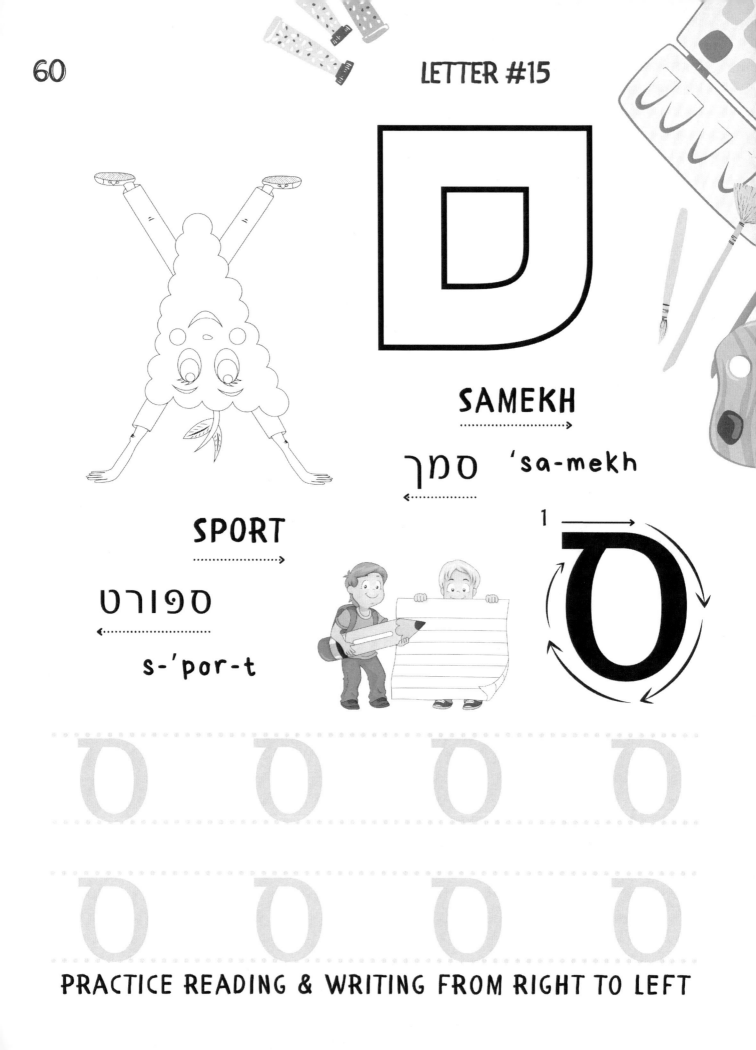

SAMEKH

סמך ʹsa-mekh

SPORT

סורט s-ʹpor-t

1

ס

PRACTICE READING & WRITING FROM RIGHT TO LEFT

LOOK AT ALL THE LETTERS YOU KNOW!

READ THEM IN ORDER - FROM RIGHT TO LEFT

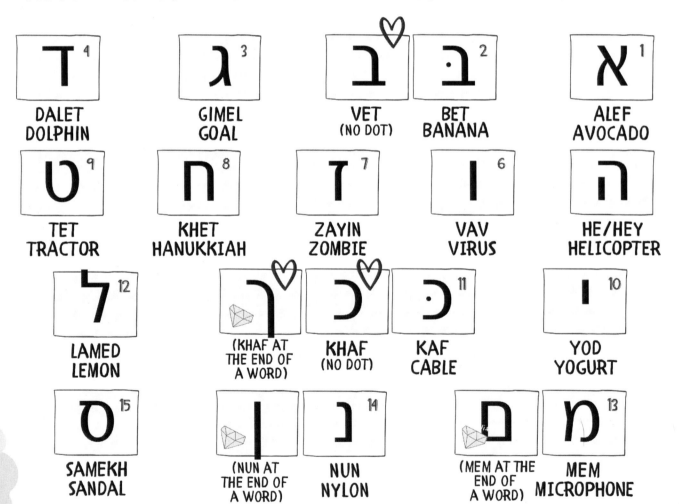

ד⁴
DALET
DOLPHIN

ג³
GIMEL
GOAL

ב
VET
(NO DOT)

בּ²
BET
BANANA

א¹
ALEF
AVOCADO

ט⁹
TET
TRACTOR

ח⁸
KHET
HANUKKIAH

ז⁷
ZAYIN
ZOMBIE

ו⁶
VAV
VIRUS

ה
HE/HEY
HELICOPTER

ל¹²
LAMED
LEMON

ך
(KHAF AT THE END OF A WORD)

כ
KHAF
(NO DOT)

כּ¹¹
KAF
CABLE

י¹⁰
YOD
YOGURT

ס¹⁵
SAMEKH
SANDAL

ן
(NUN AT THE END OF A WORD)

נ¹⁴
NUN
NYLON

ם
(MEM AT THE END OF A WORD)

מ¹³
MEM
MICROPHONE

LETTER WITH NO DUGESH (DOT REMOVED) ♡
LETTERS AT THE END OF A WORD ◇

PRACTICE YOUR LETTERS
IT'S OK TO GO BACK AND LOOK

page 42

write the letter KHAF (no Dugesh) here

page 46

write the letter LAMED here

Page 58

write the word SON (BEN) here

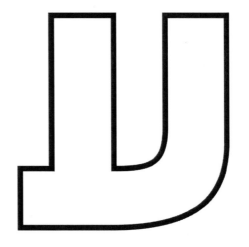

AYIN ע is one of the few letters that do not have a same sound making letter in English.
That is why we don't have a word here.

AYIN ע sounds much like the letter ALEF א, and you can say them the same

AYIN

· · · · · · · ·→

עי'ן   'a-yeen

←· · · · · · · ·

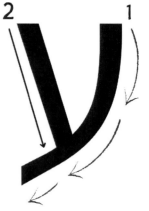

ע   ע   ע   ע   ע

ע   ע   ע   ע   ע

PRACTICE READING & WRITING FROM RIGHT TO LEFT

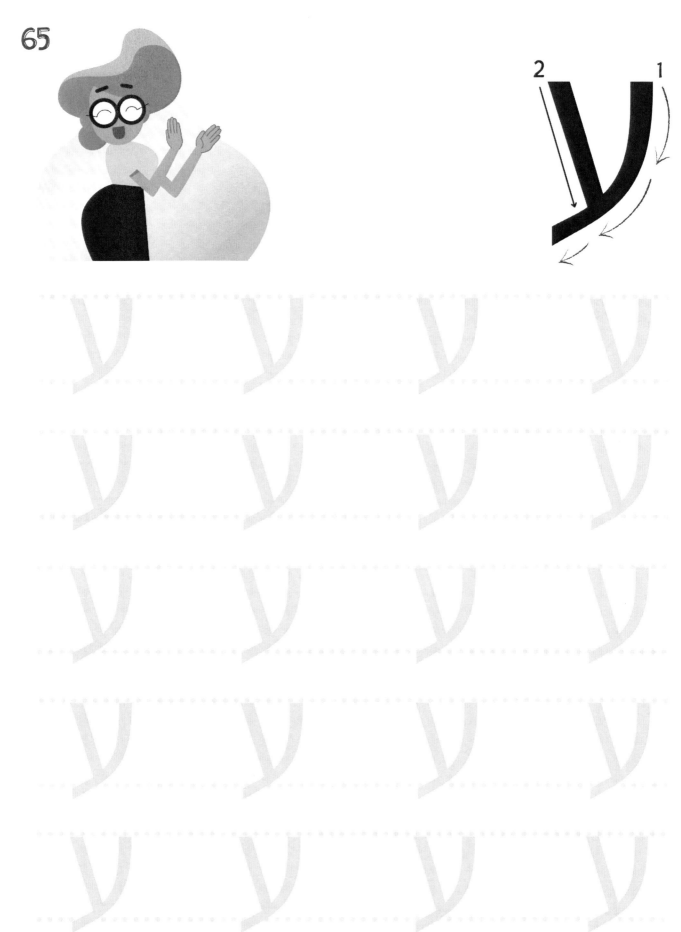

PRACTICE READING & WRITING FROM RIGHT TO LEFT

PE

פֵא   pe

PANCAKE

פַּנְקֵייק

'pan-key-k

PRACTICE READING & WRITING FROM RIGHT TO LEFT

PRACTICE READING & WRITING FROM RIGHT TO LEFT

THINGS TO KNOW ABOUT

פ

Pe

The letter PE has a variation with No Dugesh (Dot removed) called FE

פ Fe

FE פ sounds like the letter F in the word flower

PE is the third and final letter changing its sound with and without a Dugesh:

BET בּ   ב VET
KAF כּ   כ KHAF
PE פּ   פ FE

Let's practice writing FE פ

PE becomes FE when taking off its Dugesh (dot in the middle). FE sounds like F in the word Flower

PRACTICE READING & WRITING FROM RIGHT TO LEFT

THINGS TO KNOW ABOUT

ף

FE
(PE with No
Dugesh) at
the end of a
word is
written

ף

FE at the end of
a word is called
FE SOFIT.
SOFIT is the
feminine form of
the word end.

The sound of
FE פ does
not change
at the end
of a word,
only how it is
written

Let's
practice
writing
ף

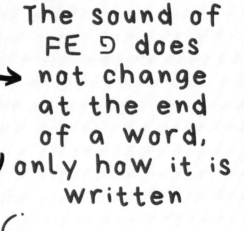

This is how we write the letter ף FE (No Dugesh) at the end of a word

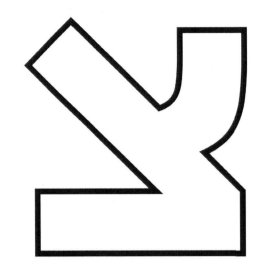

TSADI is the final
letter that does
not have a same
sound-making
letter in English.
That is why
we don't have a
word here.

TSADI makes a
Ts sound like the
z in the word
Pizza

TSADI

צַדִי 'tsa-dee

PRACTICE READING & WRITING FROM RIGHT TO LEFT

73

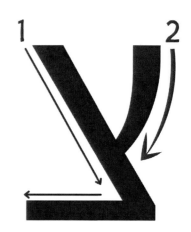

PRACTICE READING & WRITING FROM RIGHT TO LEFT

THINGS TO KNOW ABOUT

צ

TSADI צ at the end of a word is written

ץ

TSADI צ at the end of a word is called TSADI SOFIT ('tsa-dee so-'feet)

The sound of TSADI צ at the end of a word does not change, only how it is written

Let's practice writing ץ

This is how we write the letter ץ TSADI at the end of a word

ק

QOF

קוף   kof

KANGAROO

קנגורו

'ken-goo-roo

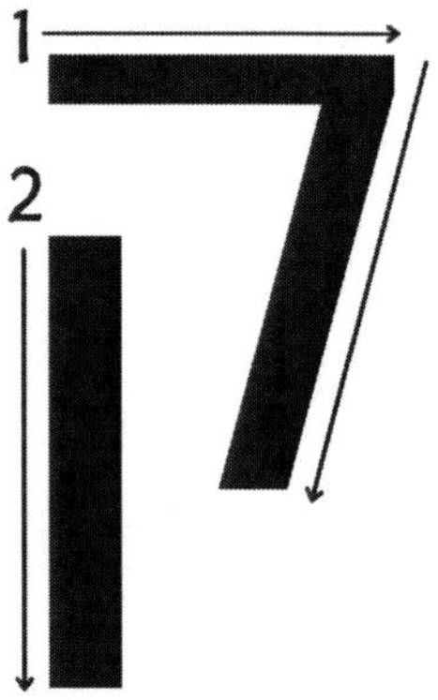

1 2 ק

LETTER #20

RESH

ר | וֹ | שׁ   resh

RADIO

רדיו

'rad-yo

1

PRACTICE READING & WRITING FROM RIGHT TO LEFT

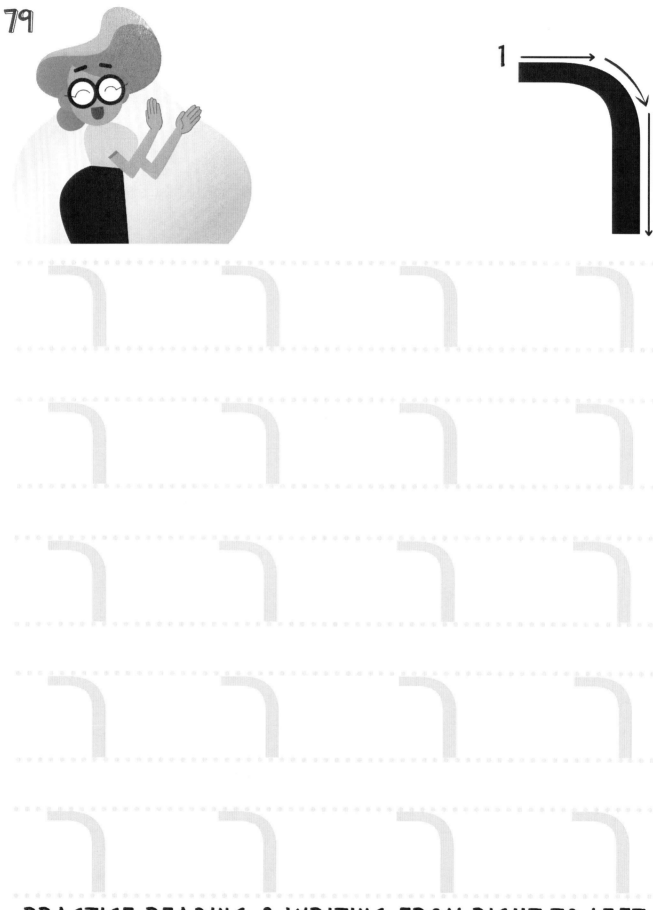

PRACTICE READING & WRITING FROM RIGHT TO LEFT

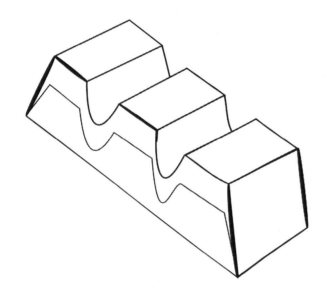

 שׁ

SHIN

שִׁין   sheen

CHOCOLATE

שׁוֹקוֹלד

'sho-ko-lad

PRACTICE READING & WRITING FROM RIGHT TO LEFT

SHIN שׁ with a dot on the top right corner makes a SH sound. This is how we write it

PRACTICE READING & WRITING FROM RIGHT TO LEFT

THINGS TO KNOW ABOUT

שׁ שׂ
SHIN

SHIN (sheen) becomes SIN (seen) by moving the dot from the top right corner to the top left

שׂ SIN

SIN שׂ makes an S sound, just like the letter SAMEKH ס you learned

Unlike the dots in the middle in the letters BET, KAF, and PE, called Dugesh, the dot in the letters SHIN and SIN is not called a Dugesh

SHIN is called Right-sided SHIN, and SIN is called left-sided SHIN, based on where the dot is placed.

SIN שׂ with a dot on the top left corner makes an S sound. This is how we write it

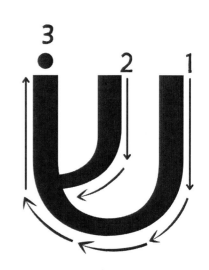

PRACTICE READING & WRITING FROM RIGHT TO LEFT

84

LETTER #22

TAV

תו tav

TEA

תה teh

PRACTICE READING & WRITING FROM RIGHT TO LEFT

PRACTICE READING & WRITING FROM RIGHT TO LEFT

YOUR NEXT WORD IN HEBREW

Now let's put together the letters BET (with a Dugesh) and TAV to write the word DAUGHTER / GIRL in Hebrew:

בַּת

Say it in Hebrew: bat

בַּת   בַּת

PRACTICE READING & WRITING FROM RIGHT TO LEFT

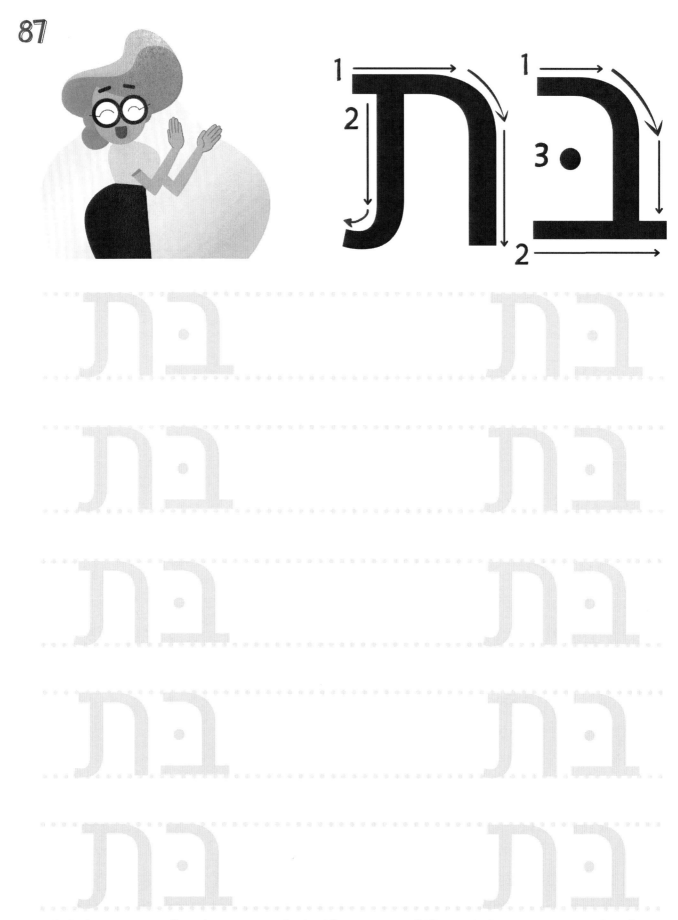

PRACTICE READING & WRITING FROM RIGHT TO LEFT

YOU KNOW THE ENTIRE ALPHABET!

DALET
DOLPHIN

GIMEL
GOAL

VET
(NO DOT)

BET
BANANA

ALEF
AVOCADO

TET
TRACTOR

KHET
HANUKKIAH

ZAYIN
ZOMBIE

VAV
VIRUS

HE/HEY
HELICOPTER

LAMED
LEMON

(KHAF AT
THE END OF
A WORD)

KHAF
(NO DOT)

KAF
CABLE

YOD
YOGURT

SAMEKH
SANDAL

(NUN AT
THE END OF
A WORD)

NUN
NYLON

(MEM AT THE
END OF
A WORD)

MEM
MICROPHONE

(TSADIK AT
THE END OF
A WORD)

TSADI

(FE AT
THE END OF
A WORD)

FE
(NO DOT)

PE
PANCAKE

AYIN

TAV
TEA

SIN

SHIN
CHOCOLATE

RESH
RADIO

QOF
KANGAROO

LETTER WITH NO DUGESH (DOT REMOVED) ♡
LETTERS AT THE END OF A WORD 💎

PRACTICE YOUR LETTERS
IT'S OK TO GO BACK AND LOOK

page 84

write the letter TAV here

page 36

write the letter YOD here

page 12

write the letter VET (no Dugesh) here

PRACTICE YOUR LETTERS
IT'S OK TO GO BACK AND LOOK

page 76

write the letter QOF here

page 80

write the letter SHIN here

page 86

write the word GIRL (BAT in Hebrew) here

YOU KNOW THE ENTIRE ALPHABET!

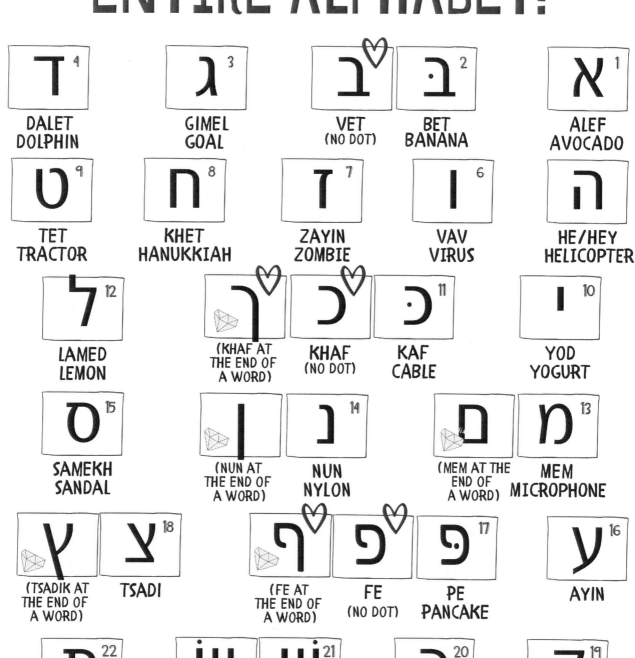

דַ 4
DALET
DOLPHIN

גַ 3
GIMEL
GOAL

בּ 2
VET
(NO DOT)

בּ 2
BET
BANANA

אָ 1
ALEF
AVOCADO

ט 9
TET
TRACTOR

ח 8
KHET
HANUKKIAH

זַ 7
ZAYIN
ZOMBIE

וַ 6
VAV
VIRUS

הַ 5
HE/HEY
HELICOPTER

לַ 12
LAMED
LEMON

ךַ
(KHAF AT
THE END OF
A WORD)

כַ
KHAF
(NO DOT)

כּ 11
KAF
CABLE

יַ 10
YOD
YOGURT

סַ 15
SAMEKH
SANDAL

ןַ
(NUN AT
THE END OF
A WORD)

נ 14
NUN
NYLON

םַ
(MEM AT THE
END OF
A WORD)

מ 13
MEM
MICROPHONE

ץַ
(TSADIK AT
THE END OF
A WORD)

צ 18
TSADI

ףַ
(FE AT
THE END OF
A WORD)

פ
FE
(NO DOT)

פּ 17
PE
PANCAKE

עַ 16
AYIN

ת 22
TAV
TEA

שַׂ
SIN

שָׁ 21
SHIN
CHOCOLATE

רַ 20
RESH
RADIO

קַ 19
QOF
KANGAROO

LETTER WITH NO DUGESH (DOT REMOVED) ♡
LETTERS AT THE END OF A WORD ◇

THIS PAGE IS BLANK
SO YOU CAN CUT-OUT
THE ALPHABET SHEET AT THE BACK OF THIS PAGE.

MOUNT IT ON THE WALL,
CARRY IT WITH YOU ON-THE-GO,
OR BRING IT TO CLASS FOR QUICK & EASY ACCESS

CONGRATULATIONS!

You've crossed your first finish line in your Hebrew journey! I hope you're super proud of your accomplishment—I know I am!

Your dedication and hard work will continue to reward you as you build upon your knowledge and reading/writing skills. By completing this workbook, you've learned the Print Alphabet letters—an essential foundation for your journey.

Your next step is to perfect your writing skills with the graceful Cursive/Script letters in the Hebrew 2 Workbook. To see fast results and avoid any frustration, it's best to start Hebrew 2 as soon as you've completed Hebrew 1 (which is... now!).

By finishing Hebrew 1 and 2, you'll complete all your writing skills in Hebrew! How exciting is that?

Your last step will be learning the vowel system called Nikud, which is all laid out and simplified for you in the Hebrew 3 textbook. As you complete these three steps, you'll have all the necessary skills to read and write in Hebrew!

Order your copies of Hebrew 2 & 3 locally at **HEBREWBYINBAL.COM/ORDER to continue your beautiful journey.**

If you haven't had the chance to leave feedback on this workbook, I'd be eternally grateful if you could take a minute to leave your review on Amazon. Your feedback will not only help others but also show your support for the effort put into creating this workbook. Thank you!

As your guide, I'm always here to offer support throughout your journey. If you have any questions, face challenges, or want to share an exciting win, please feel free to reach out to me at hi@hebrewbyinbal.com.

Use my resources, free lessons and guides, conversational courses, and more - all available on HEBREWBYINBAL.COM and @hebrewbyinbal on YouTube and across social media,

and I'll see you in Hebrew 2!

PRACTICE READING & WRITING FROM RIGHT TO LEFT

PRACTICE READING & WRITING FROM RIGHT TO LEFT

PRACTICE READING & WRITING FROM RIGHT TO LEFT

PRACTICE READING & WRITING FROM RIGHT TO LEFT

PRACTICE READING & WRITING FROM RIGHT TO LEFT